A
is for Alpaca!

Elena Stowell and Kelly Jarvis

Illustrations by

Kent A. Barichievich

Presented by:

Order this book online at www.trafford.com
or email orders@trafford.com

Most Trafford titles are also available at major online book retailers.

 www.trafford.com

North America & international
toll-free: 1 888 232 4444 (USA & Canada)
fax: 812 355 4082

Our mission is to efficiently provide the world's finest, most comprehensive book publishing service, enabling every author to experience success. To find out how to publish your book, your way, and have it available worldwide, visit us online at www.trafford.com

Because of the dynamic nature of the Internet, any web addresses or links contained in this book may have changed since publication and may no longer be valid. The views expressed in this work are solely those of the author and do not necessarily reflect the views of the publisher, and the publisher hereby disclaims any responsibility for them.

ISBN: 978-1-4120-5278-8 (sc)

Print information available on the last page.

Trafford rev. 10/16/2019

A *is for Alpaca!*

Alpacas are gentle and inquisitive animals bred for their luxurious fiber.

B *is for Bolivia.*

Alpacas come from three countries in South America: Bolivia, Chile and Peru.

C *is for cria.*

A baby alpaca is called a cria.

D *is for dam.*

The mommy alpaca is called a dam.

E is for end products.
Alpaca fiber can be used to
make beautiful garments
and blankets.

F is for fiber.
An alpaca is shorn
once a year to obtain
their raw fiber.

G is for Genus.

Similar animals are grouped together by the term genus. There are four animals in the genus "Lamas".

Llamas and alpacas are domestic, or tame, animals.

Llama

Alpaca

Vicuna and Guanaco are considered wild animals.

Vicuna

Guanaco

H is for Huacaya.

There are two types of alpacas. A Huacaya alpaca has a "teddy bear-like" appearance.
The Huacaya's fiber is crimped which makes the hairs stand up straight from the skin.

I *is for investment.*

Owning alpacas is an investment opportunity where many related expenses can be used as a tax-deduction.

J *is for judging.*

At alpaca shows, the animals are grouped by age, sex and color. They are judged based upon their fiber and body confirmation.

K is for kush.

Kushing is a relaxed position that alpacas will use when resting and chewing their cud.

L is for luster and locks.

Luster, or sheen, and tight pencil-like locks are characteristics exclusive to Suri alpacas.

M is for minerals.

Mineral salts are an important supplement for alpacas.

N is for nutrition.

An alpaca's diet is different from other livestock. Proper nutrition is vital to their health and fiber quality.

O is for Orchard grass.

Orchard grass is a mixture of various grasses which is the main forage for alpacas.

P is for pronking.

Pronking is when alpacas run, jump and play in the field.

Q is for Quechua.

The Quechuan people live in the Altiplano of South America. They were the ancestral keepers of the alpaca.

R is for registration,

Alpacas can be registered nationally based upon their DNA. Each registered alpaca is assigned their own number.

ribbons,

Ribbons are won for both halter and fiber class competitions.

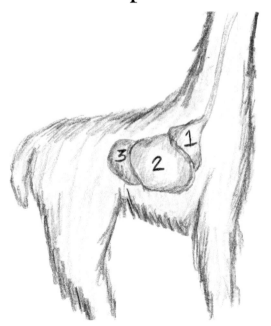

and ruminant.

Ruminants have extra stomachs that help them digest the tough grass they eat.

S is for Suri

A Suri is characterized by its long, penciled locks and a shimmery, lustrous fiber.

T *is for transport.*

Alpacas can be safely transported in a variety of vehicles such as trailers and vans.

U is for ultrasound.

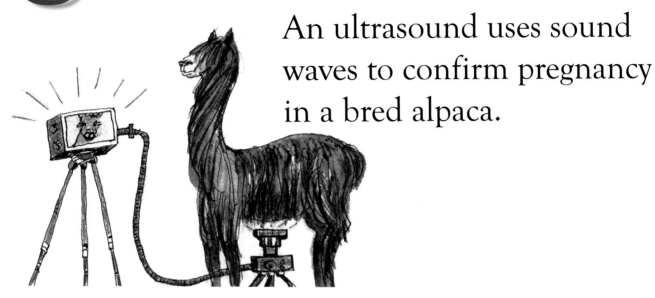

An ultrasound uses sound waves to confirm pregnancy in a bred alpaca.

V is for Vicuna.

A Vicuna is related to the alpaca. They are smaller in size and have light fawn colored fiber. Vicuna are native to South America and are considered wild animals. In Peru they are captured every two years in a "round-up" and shorn. After shearing they are released back into the wild.

W *is for weaning.*

Weaning is when the dam and cria are separated. The cria begins to eat only grass. Weaning usually occurs between 5 and 6 months of age.

Alpacas are **X** extraordinary!

exciting!

exceptional!

excellent!

expressive!

Y *is for yearling.*
After an alpaca's first birthday they are referred to as a "yearling".

Z *is for...*

z z z z z z z

Alpaca Facts

- There are over 7000 members of the Alpaca Breeders and Owners Association
- Currently, 70,000 alpacas reside in the United States
- The average alpaca weighs about 150 pounds
- Alpaca fiber is absent of guard hairs, making it soft and comfortable to wear against the skin
- There are only six teeth on an alpaca's lower jaw and none on the top jaw—they do have molars to chew their cud
- Clean up after an alpaca is a breeze since they generally deposit their waste in one area
- The feet of alpaca are soft padded and have only two toe nails
- A life span of an alpaca can be over 20 years when given proper nutrition and care
- Alpacas can hum and will chirp a warning call when startled or danger is near
- Peru is the largest exporter of alpaca products
- China is the largest importer of alpaca fiber

About the authors...

Kelly Jarvis

Residing in Maple Valley, Washington with her eleven alpacas, one llama and two dogs, Kelly is thoroughly enjoying life as an alpaca rancher. As a former biology teacher and medical assistant her life skills have been put to use caring for these amazing and inquisitive camelids. "I'm hoping this fun guide will assist all alpaca enthusiasts as they venture within the wonderful world of alpacas!"

Elena Stowell

"It's fun to put my animal science background to use." Elena earned a graduate degree in Animal Science from Washington State University where she studied ruminal fungi and made her parents proud by discovering her own (yes, it's named after her.) Currently residing in Kent, WA, Elena teaches biology and coaches youth basketball with her husband, Chuck a music teacher. She has three children, two dogs and two geckos. Some day she hopes to own a ruminant.

Kent Barichievich

Kent is an artist-at-large residing in the San Francisco area of California.

Printed in the United States
By Bookmasters